Active in organising readings and events with other poets, Elsa Korneti was born in Munich (1969), Germany, but grew up in Thessaloniki, Greece and still lives there.

She is a poet, essayist and poetry translator from English, German and Italian. Her career has been similarly diverse: studies in finance were followed by work as a journalist for well-known newspapers and magazines. She has published poetry, short stories, essays, book reviews and translations. Her screenplay under the title *White Cherry* has been distinguished and projected at the Museum of Cinematography in Thessaloniki, Greece. She organised several successful poetry slams in her city and in Athens, she inspired, organised events and brought on stage original poetic performances. She has published 15 books of poetry, short stories, essays and translations.

Her poems, short stories, book reviews, essays and translations have appeared in numerous well-known literary magazines. Part of her work among all books have been translated and published in foreign anthologies and literary magazines in ten European languages and Chinese.

Poetry
2021. Ο ήρωας πέφτει [The hero is falling] (2021). Athens: Ekdoseis ton Filon.

2021. Ξύλινη μύτη τορνευτή *[Wooden nose turned] (2021).*
Thessaloniki: Saixpirikon.

2016. Αγγελόπτερα *[Angelwings] (2016). Athens: Melani.*

2014. Κανονικοί άνθρωποι με λοφίο και μια παρδαλή ουρά
*[Normal people with a plum and a brindled tail] (2014). Athens:
Gavriilidis Edition.*

2013. Ο επαναστατικός κύριος Γκιούλιβερ *[The revolutionary Mr
Gulliver] (2013). Thessaloniki: Saixpirikon Edition.*

2012. Ο λαίμαργος αυτοκράτορας κι ένα ασήμαντο πουλί *[The
insatiable Emperor and an insignificant bird] (2012),
Thessaloniki: Saixpirikon.*

2011. Κονσέρβα μαργαριτάρι *[Tin Pearl] (2012). Athens:
Gavriilidis.*

2009. Ένα μπουκέτο ψαροκόκκαλα *[A Bouquet of Fish Bones]
(2009). Athens: Gavriilidis.*

2007. Η αιώνια κουτσουλιά *[Eternal Bird Droppings] (2007).
Gavriilidis Edition, Athens: Gavriilidis.*

2007. Στην σπείρα του κοχλία *[In the Shell's Spiral] (2007).
Thessaloniki: Malliaris.*

2017 *Eine halbe Frau? (2017), [traslated into German by Niki
Eideneier]. Frankfurt am Main: Größenwahn Verlag.*

2023. *Cómo morderás un árbol (2023), [translated into Spanish
by José Antonio Moreno Jurado]. Sevilla: Padilla Libros Editores
y Libreros, Spagna*

Essays
2013. Ημερολόγιο φιλοσοφικής ήττας *[Diary of philosophical
defeat]. Athens: (2013), Koukoutsi Pbl. Edition, Athens*

Translations
2011. *Homero Aridjis, Original title [The sun's and other poems].
(2011), Koinonia Dekaton Edition, Athens: Koinonia Dekaton
[translated from English-Spanish].*

2020. Alda Merini, Follia divina [The Divine madness].
Thessaloniki: (2020), Romi Edition Pbl., Thessaloniki [translated
from Italian].

Fiction – Prose

2020. Το νησί πάνω στο ψάρι και άλλες ευφάνταστες ιστορίες [The
island on the fish and other imaginative stories] (2020), Athens,
Melani

In loving memory of my father, Michalis and my grandmother, Veta, for the gift of storytelling.

Elsa Korneti

A BOUQUET OF FISH BONES

AUSTIN MACAULEY PUBLISHERS™

LONDON • CAMBRIDGE • NEW YORK • SHARJAH

A CIP catalogue record for this title is available from the British Library.

ISBN 9781398446205 (Paperback)
ISBN 9781398446212 (ePub e-book)

www.austinmacauley.com

First Published 2023
Austin Macauley Publishers Ltd®
1 Canada Square
Canary Wharf
London
E14 5AA

Dear incomprehension
It's thanks to you
I'll be myself at the end.
– SAMUEL BECKETT

Another Dimension

The unhappy narcissist is threatened by the loss of beauty, the sophisticate takes reward from the geometry of desires, the eccentric from defective passions, the restive spirit makes bold experiencing a series of liberating falls, the daydreamer is charmed by planetary coincidences, the womanizer falls victim to fatal attractions, the loner finds amusement "feeding" his inflated imagination with scenes of mystery. The awareness of mortality leads them to the expression of passions, perhaps even mistakes.

The carousels of all these people's little panics perpetually rotate, each circle closes for another to open and the tyranny of existence continues to be summed up in the agonizing question:

The eternality of the temporary
Or the temporary eternality?

Against a background of the universe's vast mirror, to what extent can the instantaneous, the insignificant and the random leave any trace on time's relentless flow, giving another dimension to eternality?

Water of the Ancestors

It was a time
When through the shutters of each uncontaminated day
Sprouted
A wild flower's shadow

You lived in the yard with the red cats
You rolled a silk ball
And in the evenings
Swam in a goldfish pond

In a perforated instant
Vanish
The eyewitnesses to your childhood years
There remain
The hypodermic incisions
Walking on the flesh of your soul

The astral fountain foams
In the music box
Leaving flattened shells
Remains from the entrails
Of the untimely dead star eyes

That no longer look
And froze in the frame
Remind you
That when
Almighty destiny
Strikes
You remain forced to swallow
Poisoned tears

Lesson in Balancing

The bleary-eyed light
Reposes
In a garden of deciduous daydreams

You are sitting on the yellow bike
Riding down the road with the emerald trees
Wearing a candle's tears
Emitting an anonymous glow

You turned round to look
But there was no one to watch you
And you remained alone
Rolling
On the earth's arterial roads
In the company
Of time's inarticulate cries

You just learned
To balance
On two wheels

A Heroic Deed

Say you plunged a bunch of roses
Into a vase with water of leeward silence
And washed the earth's mornings
With rain from oblivion's hair
That revives long petrified sorrows

How did you dare kiss your fate on the lips?

Who are those naughty kids
Who take aim
With their tiny slings
At God's eyes?

Darkness the Troublemaker

The darkness stares at you
With the wolf's yellow eyes

It persists in mocking you
And unperturbed goes on grinding
The day's garbage

It meticulously wipes paranoia's bleeding
Shows hospitality to memory's lightness
Attentively listens
To all the nerveless smiles

Who can bear such polished bliss?

You Left

We are
Distant and vulnerable

Droplets of the past
Remains from
Waves of dust
Scattered ashes
Left behind by
The Universe's breath,
By Eternity's passing

Acrobats
Balance
On frayed threads
Captives
In the perpetual rotation
Of the earth's axis

You just had time
To cast
A final glance
At a flaking sky
You're leaving…
Bearing
The mark
Of an incompatible age

Love's Sadism

Luminous footsteps resound in an extinguished galaxy
Dazzling flashes shatter dirty crystals
Heavy breathing quavers in excitement's well
Poisoned arrows skewer pale beds
Pores microscopic craters pour out bitter sweat
Inflated hearts gush red love
Corpulent fruits spew their juices
Flaming cells quiver
Nerves like chords vibrate
Bodies inexpugnable shells are besieged
Pillaged and abandoned in lust's maelstrom

Dishevelled waves lash the sand
Storms of heart breaking kisses paint the infinite
A sweet melody rends the clouds

"Love you fool jester"
"It's all your fault!"

Complexity

You pay for your housekeeping
To be absent.
Just as you pay for your free time
To be present.
Just as you pay for your naïve dreams.
Dearly.

*

When a little girl you chased butterflies,
As an elderly aunt reminded you.
Now only occasional longings
Fly round about you
And they're not even colourful.

*

Tell me what you prefer and I'll draw it for you.
A triangle?
A square?
A rhombus?
It's me who gives the day's shape.

Then I stand back
From a proper distance
To observe the board
With the creation – profanity.

*

You adore straying.
You deal with anything
Other than the problem.
Like that you don't solve it, you prolong it.
For you know that the routes are predetermined,
Like the lines on the shirt you're wearing.

*

How I'd love to have a simple thought
Less chaotic
Less complex
And more normal.
But who can explain to me
What "normalité" is?
Perhaps you madam?

*

It really is so difficult
To articulate I love you
Especially when you can't
Pronounce the r.

*

On the necklace the real pearls rattle
Condensing your summer desires.
When the string broke they scattered on the floor.
Once more they had no time to shine.

*

Alone the sun stands a silent accomplice
To the amorous conspiracy.
You sense them watching you.
Behind the thick foliage of passionate associations
Hide the hypocritical pretensions
All the pairs of eyes
That pounce to savage your little truths.
And as worry leads to the final outburst
Impulse malevolently lurks to see
Self-destruction triumph.

*

As a genuine docile being
With the step of a hypnotized sprite
All your life you followed the tune
Of the magic flute.
You passed
Invisible
Unnoticed
A will-o'-the-wisp
Garlanded with the circumflexes

Of a chain of illusions.

*

When you seek the cause of flight
You always stumble upon fear
The inveterate bachelor.

*

Why do you persist in digging?
Your excavations in school memories
Will bring nothing to light but
The break-up of the class
The square of the hypotenuse
And the root of 144.

*

All that green
In the colour of the dead caterpillar
Squandered on the school walls
That with complete consistency and discipline served
Then:
Blank pages
Blank minds
Now:
Blank memories
Perhaps because green is the colour of gall
And green mold.

*

You look deep in the eye
And implore for recognition and acceptance.
When will you at last accept that you've grown up?
Your wailing convinces no one listening
Because quite simply there are no listeners anymore.
Yet the rock walls do not neglect
With full responsibility
To return to you
Your muffled echo.

*

When Mr Simplicity and Mrs Complexity met
They were unsuspecting.
They travelled on a level course,
During which Mr Simplicity
Didn't understand Mrs Complexity
And Mrs Complexity suffered
From the naïve and predictable Mr Simplicity.

*

The specialist's report said:
"The complex is specific.
The simple is spontaneous and natural."
You added:
"But above all durable".

*

At least you learned albeit late
That beauty lies
Where imperfection reigns
And happiness
Where complexity
Is absent.

Furies Vs Eumenides

So fine, we cannot do it.
But nearing means distancing.
– SYLVIA PLATH

As an ardent supporter of a strange luxury
Each time your split nature celebrates
You take care to line your secrets
With silk baseness.

*

All those microscopic venomous thoughts
That accumulate in your mind
Like suspended particles
Become suicidal scorpions
That sting their heads with their tails.

*

If you're desperately trying to find
Some button on me to press
So as to live a normal life with me

Remember that my ignition point
Is inertia.

*

Pending you have
A death
That you didn't have time to mourn
And an abused relationship
That's bleeding.
Yet you're still searching for bandages.

*

I don't omit
To collect
All those gold wrappers you gave me.
Yet which were empty of candies.

*

You've got to understand
That you operate only as a receiver.
For years now the emitter
Has been shouting to you:
"Out of Order."

*

Why must you torture yourself
Torment yourself
Suffer
In order to unload all that gravel
Burdening your mind?
To sustain through artificial breathing
The corpse of the art you produce?

*

Do you know how it is to search
For someone like-minded to communicate?
And anyhow what do you have to share?
The fall of your disturbed thought?

*

Today you'll become bolder.
Every morning you throw down
The gauntlet to fight a duel
With your own cowardice.
It never takes up the challenge
But remains ensconced
In the portrait of a well-planned deceit.

*

You are never content
With what you are
With what you have
With what you do.

Your soul's swag continues
To pile up in your life's chests.
And each evening you fit inside
The thimble's cap.

*

I bow down low
Before the emotional void
And the frowning inadequacy
That you gifted me.
At your magic touch
My pathological introversion
Turned into writer's incontinence.

*

As for you who every day inhales
The fumes of your chain neuroses,
Be content with your personal confessions
To a male whore
And with your morality's incoherence.

The Familiar Polarization

I want to swim in a new soul
As blue
As carefree
As noiseless
As the sea's pregnancy.

Why should I have to endure
The sweet expectation
Of an infant deception
That preferred to abandon me
For the temporary existence
Of the yellow leaf?
Give me a reason to do so.
For one more extension of immortality?

*

By consuming yourself with illicit affairs
And serial infidelities what are you exorcising?
Old age?
Death?
How utterly mistaken you are.

Since you well know that the story always has
The same plot and the same ending.
After the voluntary exit from centre-stage
You meticulously remove the make-up
And the void again spouts from your eyes.
You have a drink together with the twin sadness-tedium.
You start to drip frozen crystals.

*

I ended up living like a solitary spool
I hang around in space
Trapped in the vortex
Of an existential delusion.
Don't worry about me though
My psychologist committed suicide tonight.

*

With interest you watch the swift step
Of the bliss
Of short-circuited brains
That leads to superficial journeys
Fertilizes felicity and gives birth to illusions
Whole lives empty cells
And a liquid anger chokes you.

*

Habit and swamps share the characteristic
Of swallowing up whatever moves.
And more and more often you fall
Into sleep's wily snare.
You always wake up drowned.

*

The tidal wave of the accumulated grief
Delivered you safe to lightness' whirl.
All you ask for now is
To exchange the gray for pink.

*

It takes an emotional nature
A great talent
And inexhaustible reserves of tears
To cry
Uncontrollably
Unstoppably
Unjustifiably.
And you are gifted.

*

After the charring of injustice at least let
The anger go up in smoke.
Give love's song a chance
To rend with its voice
The heavens' silk sheets.

31

Who Can Withstand
the Power of a Great Love

If we remove all those gold surrounds
That with their arrogant luxury
So vulgarly frame us,
We are a man and a woman
Who amid the leaves' shadows
Are creeping quietly in the dark,
We encounter the moths
Who flirt
And expect us to fall in love
Beneath a converse moon.

*

Of love there is hardly a ghost left.
O who what angel of power can assuage
My terrible demon of revenge!
You don't exist
You never existed
You were a big bite of fantasy
You are stuck to my palate
You were a egoist love

You are a ghost surpassed
Chained in a debited castle
In an attempt to save myself
From your unwanted touch
Your violent gaze
I decided to become a demon
And revenge myself on you
For all your bloodied kisses.

*

The best poem that still you haven't written
Will be about a great love that will writhe
Hanging on a question-mark's hook.

*

– And then?
– Ruined love testily brushed the dusty memories
From the lapels of forgetting and hastily dived into the red
Lizard's lair.
– And then?
– The little boy entered the room and asked:
"Mummy do red lizards exist?"

*

Then you rushed to hide.
To protect yourself from the stardust's drizzle.
That didn't touch you after all.
And you made a mistake

33

No.
You had no right to make a mistake.
Now the mistake has become your shadow
Follows you everywhere.
It becomes a pestering friend
A dependent lover
A jealous husband.

It spies on you.
Watches you.
Undresses you.

It sticks to you like a clam.
Covers you.
Gags you.
Blindfolds you.

Whatever you do you won't escape.
You find it coiling
On your fresh sheets.
Its white fang
Glints smugly in the sun.

It's a Love without love!

Mysteries and Fragments

Just as unimpeded
Your mirror's hair
Turns gray
In rehearsals that swoon
In meaningless performances
That without applause fall silent
As long as the day's clone
Remains an accident
Where the frightened ovum hides
The persistent fish
Swims against the current
Till it encounters
The reflection
Of happiness.

*

Behind bars
Silk fringes
The revolutionary brushstroke
Disintegrating dries
And longing

Gagged as it was expires
Wrapped
In a red scarf.

*

At the bottom of a glass calyx
With clay stamens
– Without any sharp objects
In your bags –
You hide
From the flying cockroaches
The nausea of the turbulence
The onslaught of wrinkles
While round about you
Unloosed
The time lost
Dries
The rose petals with the hanging whites.

*

In the perfect tale
Leading roles are played by
Imperfect people
With green winged tails
And a deep dive.

*

The human firmament's pulp
Is constantly at the right temperature
For boiling.

*

The last diamond ring
Of the aristocratic kleptomaniac aunt
Still sparkles at the pawnbroker's.

*

The family rallying over some tragedy
The loss of the tight-rope walker
The collapse of the paper tower.

*

Bizarre.
He was the first man
Who talked to you of love
Dividing it into stages
As though it were cancer.

*

And when her bright displacement
Remains one-eyed
You deceive her
Using as a pretext
The loss of beauty.

*

From the start we were too many lines
In this shape.
I withdraw quietly and silently just as
I entered
For quite simply I'm one straight line too many.

*

Learn to think
What you feel
Even when on waking
Your face
Is the foot of the rhinoceros
That passed over you in the night.

*

Let's walk in the light,
For you well know
We can't gag
A herd of rapid pulses
And the new born cry of beauty.

Eternal Bird Droppings

In the land of pleasures
There are no
Sharp corners
To injure
Your hip

The days flow
In television episodes
While in the fields
Sprout
Bills

In the horizon's fragility
Float
Lace underclothes
And pigeons
Of plexiglass

And
You
Plunging
Your sole

Into dog dirt
Left
Your tracks
On the new carpet
In the room
Of your best
Friend.

*

Fall
From an unsuccessful stunt.
Are you ready
To expose yourself
Like the eternal bird droppings
On the statue's head?

*

Just as
A drunken pigeon
Flies
Life
Flaps
Its wings
In the lens
Of the voyeur
Cinematographer.

*

Witnessing the murder
Will always be
The success
Of the idle observer
Who shows up
Uninvited
Like bird droppings.

*

The pigeons
Fly
Only
When chased
By little kids
Who wear
Bullet-proof vests.

*

At the end
Of a routine day
Winged goddesses
Fly
In the subway's carriages
While
The night shines
At the end of the tunnel.

Fade Out

I was one of the innocent and unsuspecting victims
Of a mass family hallucination.
The last kiss was not to say goodnight.
How cleverly you fooled me
Father!

*

Your life a firework that lit up and faded.
With a shove given you by God
You plummeted into infinity.
Now you're a part of the cosmic responsibility.

*

You chose your voluntary blindness.
You didn't see what was happening
As you were unable to deal with more sorrow.

But that's one more shabby excuse.

*

Shortly after one more wrong diagnosis
He'd said to you:
"That's called Leichtsinnigkeit or else
the sin of frivolity."

*

After the needle's instantaneous skipping
Came the cardiac pause.
Once your innards
Had been well gnawed
By that degenerate canker
The last word
Belonged to the cardiographer.

*

The lilt of his voice was gone for good.
Father the rock became a breeze.
Father the breakwater became a bird.
Father the thunder became a portent of rain.
He left without seeking a hug or a kiss
And remaining to divide us
Was a death and a misunderstanding.
– Why are you crying now little girl?

*

Untroubled the polar chill plundered
The unbending body
Leafed sensually through life's petals
Scattered them in the bowels
Of the pulped human firmament.
It was the last rehearsal for death.
You were present.

*

Of what use are tears?
They have nothing to wash away any more.
Yet they know how to silently creep in the dark
And hide away deep in the pillow's furrows.

*

What was lost
Is love.
Unselfish love.
And all those goodnight kisses
That evaporated in the end.

*

The diamond cross you're wearing.
His last gift to you before dying.
And to think that all his life he was an atheist.

*

You don't have the strength to repel
Sorrow's siege
When raging it knocks
At your door
When it squeezes your cells
Drains your mind
Empties your eyes
And drinks your soul.
All you can do
Is to wish it:
"Good health."

*

Lord how coldly and forcibly
You pin the absences
On the lost property board.

*

All that you wanted to say
All that you wanted to find time to say
Remained broken fish bones
Stuck in your throat.

*

You asked:
Where do all those people without shadows go?
Where do all those shadows without people go?
Where do all those people without voices go?

Where do all those voices without people go?
In the realm of silence and absence
There are
Neither bodies
Nor shadows
Nor voices.

Just before dying
He'd said to you:
"All things come to an end."

A Superfluous Truth

I wonder
Do you dream of me?
As a drop of wax
Or a splash of milk?

*

Freckles
Summer trophies.
Hers.
Freckles
Stimulant pills.
His.

*

You like
What's uncoordinated after all
To be dazzled
By fairy lights
To stuff yourself
With adjective cookies

47

When you are in poetic ecstasy

*

The kiss you once gave me
I keep
As a lifebelt.

*

Betrayal's rags
Clothe remorse
With haute couture
Selections.

*

The red bow
Decorates sobriety's pump
And the Guinea fowl's head.

*

In order to successfully unblock
The pipe of your vocal chords
All you need do is blow
Into a daisy's throat

*

I had to meet you
On the back of a playing card
To learn
That a Royal Flush
Is not a matter of good luck
But of clever bluffing.

*

Without your having time
To savour "all"
You found yourself with "nothing".
The loss of your story
Was simply the product
Of a glutted memory.

*

It's never too late
To learn to give
Gratuitous embraces
And to search
For accommodating truths.

*

Have you at all considered
That the animal you're wearing
Constitutes by itself
A statement of luxury?

*

Are you ready to go out into the storm
To pack it up
In cases and boxes?

*

Since everything is
Under total supervision
It's high time
You devoted yourself
To something uncontrolled.

*

The conquest of loneliness
Is your social success.

*

Your life's weathervane
Is constantly turned
In the direction
Of the half-measure.

*

The worst feeling:
To know that they're aware of
Your ignorance.

*

The meaning of your existence
Was summed up in eugenics.

[14 Transformations]
Passion's Journal

1

Fresh passion
Just before you squeeze it
Completely round
Succulent and incalculable
As to the juice's loss

2

In relationships' intensive care
Eternally under treatment
As an emergency case
Is love's disease

3

In the marriage of fire and water
Prevalent is the extremity that
Wavers between the
Disorder of Hell

And the disturbance of Heaven

4

And yet
When you leave
Your body
Adrift
In the tempest
And your mind
The lighthouse's captive
Passion
A conscious decision
Remains

5

Love's contest
Leads you to one more successful
Crystal-shattering attempt
You can no more cancel
The scars from the fragments
They embed themselves in you
Are transformed
Into lively lepidoptera

6

A happy love
Is a tragic love

7

When the mysterious power
Of a fatal attraction strikes
Out of compassion
The fin
Of the shark
Passes you by

8

The penultimate passion
Like the penultimate mistake
Provides the opportunity
For one more last time

9

Don't worry.
Love's passion
First
By fair means
Corrupts you

10

After hammering you
In earnest
It cast you unconscious
In the forest glade
You get up

Accustomed
Helpless
Imperfect

11

Passion
As a romantic technocrat
Consumes itself in
An ennobled
And methodical delirium
In the end
With relief
It spits
The heart's pip
Into an ashtray
Coloured pink

12

You must have read
The prayers wrongly
Because when
Balancing between
Heaven and Hell
You invoked Him
The God of Spirits
Appeared

13

In the futility
Of soulless love
The bodies
Vibrate
With vulgarity
To pornography's rhythm

14

After the rubbing of the bodies
The wager in a passionate relationship:
To emerge unscathed
From the flames
In order to proclaim
Your existence once more

passion's epilogue

When the passion of excess
Seizes you
Passion's journal
Becomes a journal of flesh
With a lens's instant motion
The eye captures
What never existed

The Interminable Digestion of Angelic Terror

1

Imperfect perfection
Decay's decline
Destruction's fluidity
Existence's delirium
Constitute the recipe
For the sensual enjoyment
When I eat YOU
When you eat ME

2

I'll devour you
You'll devour me
I'll savage you
You'll savage me
At a feast for starving beasts
We'll eat each other
We'll digest each other
So as to remain

Two strangers
The one
Inside the belly
Of the other

3

The persistent quest
In the depths of black
With borrowed angel's wings
Elevates you
Ever higher
To the surface of the
Superficial water

4

The decomposition of desire
Put the tedium in surprise
The fear of loss
The surprise in tedium
When as a birthday gift you find
Wedged in your pillow
A petrified
Peach

5

In a society of predators
Where can a rabbit hide
To escape?

Its burrow
Is not as deep
As it ought to be

6

Stop terrifying me
I'm not scared of you
A poor and defenseless
Demon
Is all you are

7

Come
Let's fly together
To the summit of the night
We'll be hurled
By the lightning's vertigo

Brancousi's Egg

I

The woman suspended between the cast and the wall
The man captive in the outline

Come then
Make a move
While the voice still caresses the look

The woman is hatched in the cast

You know you can do it
Break with the format

The cast grows larger
The slit gets narrower

Say something
Break with the trite

Behind the gate
He stares at her puzzled
Trying to understand

To understand?

Outside the cast the woman
Cracks

> Don't stare at me
> Make a revelation
> Search for an intervention

The wave dyes the toes a saffron colour

The woman lies beneath the cast
The plaster body empty
An oval shell
Without markings

The words compose themselves in explanation
As the object moves away
The emptiness of the space grows larger

A man will appear with whom she'll fall in love
But not yet

II

The egg or the bird
Question?
The bird or the egg
> The perfect oval bird flies
> The sense of flying?

The bird the egg the bird
Obsession?
The egg the bird the egg

     The perfect oval face reclines
     The flight of matter?

The answer is to be found
            On white walls
When you wear a pair
Of blackened eyes
No, the answer is to be found

     In black photos
When you wear the walls
As a shell

Wrong again, the best answer is to be found

     On white walls where
     Black photos are hanging

In black photos I tell you

No, I've thought about it again, on white...

"Don't worry, I'm fine," he said
Putting a glass of wine to his lips

And then
     The rattles came

No
And then
      Came the suspicion
That the poet is perhaps
Drunk

III

In the riddle's return there is
A shallow course giving a final opportunity to the bee's
Sting
A shallow compromise
                Binds you with a rusty safety pin
A shallow end
                Is blocked by an annoying bush
A stale dispute that smells

Just before finding that it was light
                Just before its perfect outline cracks
And it's eventually discovered
That to blame for everything was:
                The egg
                The rotten egg

Two Semi-Circles

1st semicircle
Gaining the half

2nd semicircle
Struggling for the other half

Circle
The result that you always lose the whole
The python
The python circle
The python circle noose

The cordon of imaginary enemies
Encircles you
Tightens round you
Till it suffocates you
And then dresses you
In a shiny snakeskin shirt
With gold scales

Yes.
For the first time I notice the asphyxiation
I see that asphyxiation has a color
Asphyxiation is gold
Gold and measurable
A full 18 carats
Persistently grind your finger
Teaching you
To stoically endure
Successive distortions
And to amuse yourself
With all the opposite
Imperfect
Yet inseparable pairs of things
To understand why
Right fights against right
And not wrong

You know it anyway
It's the law of the ocean
When hypocrisy heightens mirth
The coupling takes place on the reef
For safety
The self-preservation instinct
So powerful
Between two pains
You always choose the lesser
You call it the right to less

Yet how do you admit love's absence
And the unknown personal stigma?

Why don't you at last accept it
The communication channel has for some time
Taken the course of the drains

And when they ask you:
"How does escape translate today?"
You reply:
"Why, as creative anxiety."

You strive to leave behind you a nonplussed crowd
A swarm of horseflies that will stare at you
As you walk away
All these are
Toxic people
Toxic live-in spouses

All those are
The gum stuck to the tulip's petals
The toothpaste tube's open cap
That cries out
Cries out
But who can hear the tube's voice?
It's crumpled
Petrified

In Verona'a arena
The terrible lizard
Curls like a ring
Content
In order to digest

You're enchanted by its castrato voice
"What's it singing?"

"The wedding ring's bite."

Sleeping Beauty

It's a strange feeling
To see your body
When you're sleeping
As a spectator

My dear audience

I'm sorry but in this performance
I can't even move,
I'd like so much to play
Once again the role
Of my favorite Drama Queen
Who for days has been painting
On a red and black background
A la maniere d' El Greco

Yet I think that the fact
That I exist as an absence
By itself provides
An exceptional staging

Please don't cry –
At the height of their beauty
Blooming roses shed their petals

There remains the interminable journey
Without destination
And you
Faithful
To your incestuous relationship
With perfection

No,
You didn't want the cloth heart
It shrinks in the wash
Nor the metallic one
It rusts
You preferred the glass one
The most reliable material
Whatever happens,
Whether it breaks or cracks,
It remains clear, transparent

Now stoically you wait
For an angel to fall
Like an overly ripe grape
From a cloud bunch
To tie you to its wing
And save you

Do you see:
Frame by frame the sky is rotting
For you to count leaks and damp
First you had to become dead inside
To give away to the unfortunate
Your dead father's designer ties
How many more times will you be asked
To confess your innocence?
Only the glass heart's bells
Inhabit you
Dissonantly
So dissonantly
They resound
Without sound

You'd told them:
I never asked to be awakened
And they all insist on waking me
I never asked for an antidote
And they all insist on giving me to drink
Nor did I ever ask
For the Blue Prince's kiss
And they all insist on kissing me

You've accepted it for some time
Women can't read maps
Women get lost
At least you're in no danger
You're always here
Pinned down
Pinned down

Pinned down
Horizontally
The tragic longing creeps up
Its tentacles
Enfold you
Tightly, methodically

Your clock cries:
"Get up!
It's Gucci time!
Waiting for you is the black limousine
And a tiger in your bed."

Mural

On Jackson Pollock's canvas

It's another life
It wraps you tight each evening
Printed on a strip of paper

When you're asleep you hold on
To a butterfly's broken leg
Like that you feel less wretched
You're used now to tolerating
The broken words

The lovely blue passion
Withdrew
The spattered shoes
Walk on the canvas
The white landscape melts

You wonder:
"What does the unusual taste like?"
Once again
You persist in focusing
On the cheekbones' flawless anatomy

"But you promised me you'd think less."
"I can't," you say, "it's the sun that whispers
The hot air in my ear."

In a careful groping of cracks
You faithfully follow the brushstrokes
Left on the mural
By the instant attraction

Ragman
From opportune betrayals
The alien body hosts you
Out of necessity

Desperately you seek limpidity
But remain enclosed in the
Cloud
"How can you be so
Sought after and alone at the same time?"

First image:
The couple
Arms outstretched
Welcome you
So you'll enter into the spirit of the role

Second image:
The persecution
The loss
The arms
In a reverse circular motion

A clock without hands
Spells out hours washed away

A strange desire
Your body confuses you
The wrapping is you see
Flashy
To your surprise you realize
That the body is missing

You memorized the inadequacy
Now you seek generous compensation
For the anorgasmic years

You think
That you have need of
A bold and desperate act of resistance
(Against death?)

Third image:
Get undressed now!
Let's not waste time

The sound of the rain
On the leaves
The powder of the kiss
In the shape of a half-moon

The wind
The water
Do you feel them?

Panting
Flows in your eyes
Two fluffy clouds
Copulation
On the bottom of a blue can

There she is! Do you see her?

The moon woman
The moon woman breaks the circle

The word left unsaid
Will have to be said
To elevate
The poetic perversion
To eternity

"Do you love me?"

Tomorrow

Donna Anna:
"I wish I had the strength to hate
But we must part."
Don Juan:
"When shall we meet again?"
Donna Anna:
"Another time?"
Don Juan:
"Tomorrow?"
– LORENZO DA PONTE

Velvet befits the darkness
What about silk?
Lace perhaps?
Yes, lace!
The image of the perforated
The holes
Open mouths gaping
Hospitable
They allow the cold to pass
Perhaps slightly immoral
Unpredictable

Especially when they become misshapen
The holes in long lace sleeves
Countless tiny black eyes
How piercingly they stare at you
Eyes masks
Velvet eyes masks
How persistently you wore them
Yet they don't belong to you, they are
Borrowed
Borrowed eyes
Borrowed eyes velvet masks
However many you wear
You can't hide from
The cracks in your self
The mirror's explosions
The touches of others
When from your body pulling
Silk threads
They slowly and deviously unravel you
You come apart
You lose the predator's glow
Gazing over the valley of lost loves
Your tongue retains the taste of chaos:

"Guardandomi allo specchio ni metto a ridere"
"ha ha ha ha ha ha ha ha ha ha ha ha ha ha ha."

Looking in your mirror you laugh
Looking from your window you age
Looking at the crowd you fear
A crowd of people lances
Awaits your irreversible step

Greed is punished
With more devilish intercourse
With a female punch
With a male kick
Remember before leaving to tidy the room
Every now every later
Remember to again plan the vulnerable room
That you might re-define yourself
Remember to return the stolen hearts
That you might with passion begin to live each dead day
Under a strange delusion

As a genuine acrobat of desire
Just before returning to your wet destiny
You shout to them:

        "Hypocrites!
        Pretend!"

Just before falling you shout to her

        Tomorrow my love!
        Tomorrow!

                                    – Venice, October 2007

Outer-Plating

The elderly lady
One hundred years of age
With the black scales
With the invincible bone plating
Basks peaceful in the sun

Waiting in vain to soar
She realizes that her watery world
Remains subterraneanly stable
She often considers that
It requires great craft in order
For her to withstand the overflow
Of invisible volumes of water
It requires great talent
For her to deviously creep up
On every prospective meal
Great repute in order
For her to be proclaimed
The notorious carnivorous reptile
That time favours more than the vultures
A mother's great heart in order
For her to conceal her descendants

In the water lilies

Yet she can
In a recollection of innocence
Blunt
The edge of a nettle
Live searching for
One more dreamy association
As she sinks
In the priceless gift
Of the deluge

She can
Allow them all
The curious, the astounded
To ask her:

Do you have anything more to add?
A crocodile tear
Perhaps?

Sea Demon

Look at me please
This is my new carnival outfit
This year I dressed as a sea chandelier

Snake hair undulates on my brow
Inward electrified cables
Crystal head a magnifying glass
So I can gaze with the water a prism
At the infinite from the seabed
So I can be a blue star
A self-satisfied wheel that endlessly rolls
Around itself

There's a way for me to conquer him
To swallow him whole
To digest his bones

With body a hydraulic pump
A bell that whines
I become a fearsome monster
And stick like a sucker
To the face

No comb
Brushes me
Whoever touches me
Is paralyzed

I'll love
Whoever finds me
Whoever without turning to stone
Gazes at me

Me
The Toxic Gorgon Medusa
Who pollutes the ocean
Like a blue
Plastic
Bag

Destroy Van Gogh

I'm just 33 yet breaking down
How long does the deconstruction last?
While I'm falling apart
The ants are emptying my mind
Marvel at me as a corpse then
An ideal *nature morte*
Skull clad in seaweed
I'll give it a cigarette to smoke
If I were a headless body?
Perhaps I'd escape the asylum
What's to blame? Absinth? Whores?
All the dark women in my life
Wear black
Come out of illusion – Get into reality
Impossible – I married the green fairy
Every night she becomes a demon and then a snake –
The snake bites its tail – becomes a woman's vagina
It drowns me in the wet channel
I live in the beloved triangle
Between three lines
Does the demon command you?
It inspires me

It kills you

At least let's save what still exists between us

Love should be noiseless

But I don't know you in order to love you

Change yourself – Get yourself together

I adore untidiness

You're doomed

F a t h e r I'm sorry

Now I know

That's how I was born

I live to paint perfection with madness

Madness with perfection

I'm tired – I want to snuggle in the roomiest

Bird's nest in my collection – torpor is a nice word –

I promise never to defend my disability again

Winged Poetesses

Ladies and gentlemen
I'd like to confess my addiction
I'm a kleptomaniac
I steal the oxygen from words
I inhale their voices
Because only like this can I breathe
Your turn now:
Ladies and gentlemen
I'd like to confess my addiction
I'm suicidal
I collect my prospective deaths
Like cats do their lives
I have seven whole deaths to live
Leave her at last
To undress in peace
The bodies are expressionless
I declare myself an enemy of movement
Yet more and more often
I fall, fall…
Take note
On the dividing line stands
The rival lover – The rival beloved

Stoically they wait with hooked noses
The male always the first to smell fertility
Help – I remember nothing
The stolen moments don't last long
I hate my intuition
Step this way please
Cheap sunsets sold here
I gift you
My accursed beauty
On mauve paper
And I gift you
My accursed mind
In a mauve box
Vanitas – The name of our punishment
After every heavy drinking bout
We remain ever more thirsty
Yet eventually we'll be pinned to the sky
Like two huge Attacus Atlas butterflies
Our deaths
Will be a mere detail

Beloved

The yellow cubes
Hang
Held by a red thread of blood
Blind butterflies
Surge though
The heart's trapdoor
The body sawed in drawers
Beautiful desirable
He hovers
Before the plague

Its spreading
Is a matter of time
The brave man
With humble square nails
Generously Ruthlessly
Was riddled
With the sewing-machine's stitches
Of death
Suspended
His constellation
Finds its place

In the resplendent cosmos
To remain unharmed
And whole
Boundless love
Left us alone to struggle
With how to surpass
The wretched self

Just sign please
And then cast your mite

"In the slot, in the yellow box
In the shape of a cross
Thank you all," said Salvador Dali
Stepping away
From the Crucifixion

Eve's Navel

Do you remember your words on stage?

Sorry but memorizing was never one of my talents

Let's begin then
With a circular not linear sentiment
With a blemished and misshapen rose
I'd undergo any humiliation
To be part
Of this dream.
Yet, what a shame!
I can't hold a paintbrush
Dreams! I can't touch them
When simply at the touch they commit suicide
But I promise to respect the words
Especially those that bury absences

You said to me:

It depends
Whether you sleep
To forget
Or to remember

Joining all the direct connections
Between chance events I ended up living in
A colony of microbes
A blue water-lily
Sprouted in the dot
Of the question mark
When it pierced
The middle of my belly
My mind is a room with a garden
Sitting in its centre is Eve
She rolls and unrolls her navel
Weaving a braid of rolling ruin
A procession of crabs
Holding tightly by their claws
So you can't tell if they're helping
Or quarrelling with each other

Now the cord is hanging helpless
A red alert that flashes
You hear her calling:
Can someone please sew my button?

Translated from Greek to English by David Connolly

The Translator

David Connolly (translator) was born in 1954 in Sheffield and is of Irish descent. He studied ancient Greek at the University of Lancaster and medieval and modern Greek literature at Trinity College, Oxford before gaining a PhD from the University of East Anglia on the theory and practice of literary translation. He has lived in Greece since 1979 and became a naturalized Greek citizen in 1998. He was Head of Translation at the British Council in Athens from 1991 to 1994, and lectured in literary translation at the Ionian University from 1991 to 1997 and at the University of Athens from 1999 to 2000. He has more recently taught at the Aristotle University of Thessaloniki. Connolly's translated anthology *The Dedalus Book of Greek Fantasy* won the Hellenic Society's Modern Greek Translation Prize for 2004. His translations have won awards in Greece, the UK and the USA. http://www.enl.auth.gr/staff/connolly/

"The maturity of Elsa Korneti's voice testifies years of silent craft and an impressive familiarity with modern world poetry. Hers is a personal poetry, yet it deals with themes universally relevant and does so in a disarmingly sincere and unpretentious way. The dialog between a critical alter ego and the self-reveals whatever false, deceptive, concealed, but also whatever true and valuable there may be in the narrator's experiences. Elsa Korneti is an exciting voice in Contemporary Greek Poetry".

(David Connolly, Professor Emeritus,
translator
Department of Literature and Translation,
Aristotle University of Thessaloniki Greece)

"Elsa Korneti is a Greek writer of great range and depth. She is a prolific poet, fiction writer, essayist, critic, translator, and cultural activist whose presence is felt across many literary domains. She moves between late Modernism and advanced Postmodernism and loves to experiment in terms of both forms and themes. She draws on a wide variety of genres, from folk tale and fable to science fiction and children's literature to explore their tradition and survival. She mobilizes a wide variety of styles, such as allegory,

dystopia, and parody, producing a consistently polyphonic writing. Her intertextual breadth ranges from Greek myth to cinematic symbolism. She incorporates insights from fields such as history, sociology, philosophy, aesthetics, and feminism. EK's learning, imagination, craft, and ideas are combined to address the challenges of the 21st century."

– Vassilis Lambropoulos
C.P Cavafy Professor Emeritus of Modern Greek
Departments of Comparative Literature and Classical
Studies
University of Michigan

"Korneti's tireless experimentations with form unleash the workings of imaginative resistance to what she has described as the "technocratization" of contemporary life, the market-driven, consumer logics that pervade human experience today, from the digitization of such experience to the economies and geopolitical trials and tribulations of globalization. For Korneti, poetry's triumph of conscience, its defense of the human condition, is not so much evident in the grand revolt or the broadly political narrative, but in the recuperation of the myriad small gestures of defiance that testify to the freedom and vitality of the poetic imagination."

– Patricia Felisa Barbeito
Professor of American Literatures at RISD
Rhode Island Providence

"Elsa Korneti was nominated on the National Poetry Awards Short List twice (2009, 2011). She moves steadily

towards a field of scholarly poetry, intertwining her personal experience with a wealth of cultural influences and often, with the characteristics of feminist intention.

With thoughtful linear thinking, Korneti assesses the lives of others, at the same moment when she exposes her own with a voice that's heard from the depths of her poetic interaction with postmodern poets, at the same time, when her poetic world is structured with composure on the expression of the universal female experience, bypassing any ethnic or social commitment.

In other words, we could say that Korneti creates a speaker who bears only one identity that of gender which contemplates its nature and its position. And in this continuous, but not at all random, contemplation, Korneti manages to capture and extend her poems, leaning onto the foundations of the universal human and the world."

– Eleni Tzatzimaki
Literature critic, poet,
PhD scholar at Sorbonne University

9 781398 446205